YOU'RE PART OF
FAMILY
COMMUNITY!

T0009990

BY THERESA EMMINIZER

Gareth Stevens
PUBLISHING

Please visit our website, www.garethstevens.com. For a free color catalog of all our high-quality books, call toll free 1-800-542-2595 or fax 1-877-542-2596.

Library of Congress Cataloging-in-Publication Data

Names: Emminizer, Theresa, author.
Title: You're part of a family community! / Theresa Emminizer.
Description: New York : Gareth Stevens, [2020] | Series: All our communities
   | Includes index.
Identifiers: LCCN 2019017372| ISBN 9781538245293 (pbk.) | ISBN 9781538245316
   (library bound) | ISBN 9781538245309 (6 pack)
Subjects: LCSH: Community life–Juvenile literature. | Families–Juvenile
   literature. | Communities–Juvenile literature.
Classification: LCC HM761 .E46 2020 | DDC 307–dc23
LC record available at https://lccn.loc.gov/2019017372

Published in 2020 by
Gareth Stevens Publishing
111 East 14th Street, Suite 349
New York, NY 10003

Copyright © 2020 Gareth Stevens Publishing

Designer: Sarah Liddell
Editor: Theresa Emminizer

Photo credits: cover, pp. 1, 21 Monkey Business Images/Shutterstock.com;
background texture used throughout april70/Shutterstock.com; papercute texture
used throughout Paladjai/Shutterstock.com; p. 5 pixelheadphoto digitalskillet/
Shutterstock.com; p. 7 StockImageFactory.com/Shutterstock.com; p. 9 Soloviova
Liudmyla/Shutterstock.com; p. 11 antoniodiaz/Shutterstock.com; p. 13 bearinmind/
Shutterstock.com; p. 15 Rawpixel.com/Shutterstock.com; p. 17 sonya etchison/
Shutterstock.com; p. 19 wavebreakmedia/Shutterstock.com.

Printed in the United States of America

Some of the images in this book illustrate individuals who are models. The depictions
do not imply actual situations or events.

CPSIA compliance information: Batch #CW20GS: For further information contact Gareth Stevens, New York, New York at 1-800-542-2595.

CONTENTS

Boldface words appear in the glossary.

What Is a Family?

Families come in all shapes and sizes. Some live together and some don't. Some have many members and others, just a few. Most importantly, a family is a group of people taking care of each other. Each member has a special **role** to play.

Your Family Community

A community is a group of people living and working together. Each family is its own little community. What does your family community look like? Members of your family community might be your parents or stepparents, sisters or brothers, grandparents, and you!

A Family's Needs

Each family has its own set of needs. Members of the family community work together to meet these needs. Some needs are **practical**, such as a place to live and food to eat. Other needs are **emotional**, such as feeling understood.

Family Roles

Each person within the family has their own **unique** role. Adults are **responsible** for **providing** food and a home for the family. They do this by working, paying bills, and buying food and household supplies. Children have their own roles to play too.

Where Do You Fit?

What is your role within your family community? No matter how old or young you are, you have something unique to **contribute**. You can work to meet your family's practical needs by helping out with jobs around the house.

Lend a Hand

There are simple things you can do each day to contribute to your family community. You could help cook dinner, set the table, wash the dishes, or take out the trash. You could help keep your home neat by cleaning up your room.

Do you have a little brother or sister? Part of your role could be helping take care of your younger **siblings**. If your family has a pet, you could help by feeding it or taking it for a walk.

Be Kind

You can also help meet your family's emotional needs. This is easy—show you care! When a family member is talking, listen carefully. When you have time together, make it fun! Play games and read books as a family.

How to Be a Good Member

Your family needs you, and you need them! Being a good member of a family community means being there for one another. Everyone has something special to contribute. What are some more ways that you can help meet your family's needs?

GLOSSARY

contribute: to give something to help a person, group, or cause

emotional: having to do with feelings

practical: having to do with real-life things

provide: to give

responsible: having the job of dealing with or taking care of something or someone

role: the part a person plays

siblings: brothers or sisters

unique: one of a kind

FOR MORE INFORMATION

BOOKS

Nagle, Jeanne. *Let's Find Out! Communities: What Is a Community?* New York, NY: Britannica, 2018.

Rotner, Shelley, and Sheila M. Kelly. *Families*. New York, NY: Holiday House, 2015.

WEBSITES

Kids Health
kidshealth.org/en/kids/parents.html?WT.ac=ctg#cathome-family
Learn more ways to show your family you care.

Women and Children's Health Network
cyh.com/HealthTopics/HealthTopicDetailsKids.aspx?p=335&np=282&id=1791
Learn more about getting along with your family.

INDEX